SOUTH AFRICA

By Sloane Gould
and Kate Shoup

EXPLORING WORLD CULTURES

Cavendish Square

Published in 2024 by Cavendish Square Publishing, LLC
2544 Clinton Street, Buffalo, NY 14224

Second Edition

Website: cavendishsq.com

Cataloging-in-Publication Data

Names: Gould, Sloane, author. | Shoup, Kate, author.
Title: South Africa / Sloane Gould, Kate Shoup.
Description: Second edition | Buffalo, New York: Cavendish Square Publishing, 2024. | Series: Exploring World Cultures | Includes glossary, index, and bibliographic information
Identifiers: ISBN 9781502667540 (pbk) | ISBN 9781502667557 (library bound) | ISBN 9781502667564 (ebook)
Subjects: LCSH: South Africa-- Juvenile literature
Classification: LCC DT1719 G68 2024 | DDC 968--dc24

Writers: Kate Shoup; Sloane Gould (second edition)
Editor: Caitie McAneney
Copyeditor: Shannon Harts
Designer: Andrea Davison-Bartolotta

The photographs in this book are used by permission and through the courtesy of: Cover Monkey Business Images/Shutterstock.com; p. 4 mark reinstein/Shutterstock.com; p. 5 WOLF AVNI/Shutterstock.com; p. 6 Ondrej Bucek/Shutterstock.com; p. 7 Bardocz Peter/Shutterstock.com; p. 8 Internet Archive Book Images/Flickr; p. 9 File:Robert Sobukwe leads anti-apartheid protest (cropped).jpg/Wikimedia Commons; p. 10 Nova Photo Works/Shutterstock.com; p. 11stephane lalevee/Shutterstock.com; p. 13 (bottom) Krakenimages.com/Shutterstock.com; p. 13 (top) Villiers Steyn/Shutterstock.com; p. 14 Therina Groenewald/Shutterstock.com; p. 15 Art Konovalov/Shutterstock.com; p. 16 Codegoni Daniele/Shutterstock.com; p. 17 Benny Marty/Shutterstock.com; p. 18 Rich T Photo/Shutterstock.com; p. 19 Richard Cavalleri/Shutterstock.com; p. 20 Sunshine Seeds/Shutterstock.com; p. 21 Grobler du Preez/Shutterstock.com; p. 22 View Apart/Shutterstock.com; p. 23 Dendenal/Shutterstock.com; p. 24 Kathy Hutchins/Shutterstock.com; pp. 25, 29 MD_Photography/Shutterstock.com; p. 26 Carlo Kaminski/Shutterstock.com; p. 27 Paolo Bona/Shutterstock.com; p. 28 BBA Photography/Shutterstock.com.

CPSIA compliance information: Batch #CS24CSQ: For further information contact Cavendish Square Publishing LLC at 1-877-980-4450.

Printed in the United States of America

CONTENTS

INTRODUCTION

South Africa is a country of **diversity**—in its wildlife, landscapes, and people. Here you'll find zebras, rhinoceroses, and cheetahs, as well as African penguins. With 11 official languages and people of many **ethnic** backgrounds, South Africa has a unique mix of cultures, or beliefs and ways of life. In fact, a famous **archbishop** named Desmond Tutu called it the "rainbow nation," as this name describes its colorful blend of cultures.

In 1994, Nelson Mandela was elected as the first Black president of South Africa.

Located in southernmost Africa, this area has a long history. People have lived there for hundreds of thousands of years. Europeans started taking over the land in the 17th century, leading to **injustice** against the Black people there. Black South Africans didn't have the same rights as white South Africans and had to live separately. In the past 30 years, however, South Africa has given equal rights to all.

Many people visit South Africa to see wildlife.

GEOGRAPHY

Found at the very tip of Africa, South Africa has a long coast. One part of the coast is by the Atlantic Ocean. The other is by the Indian Ocean. The two oceans meet around Cape Point, at the tip of South Africa's Cape **Peninsula**.

The Great Escarpment splits the country in two. An escarpment is a steep hill. Along the bottom of the hill is the country's coastal region. The Cape Fold Mountains cover part of this area. Wild animals like lions, rhinoceroses, and giraffes can be found west of the Lebombo Mountains. A large plateau, or flat area, is on top of the escarpment.

This is the Drakensberg, the eastern part of the Great Escarpment.

FACT!

South Africa is nearly twice the size of Texas.

This map of South Africa shows its major cities and the surrounding countries.

The Kalahari Desert to the north is a sandy **savanna**. It's home to wildebeest and antelope called springboks.

A NATION WITHIN A NATION

South Africa has a whole country within its borders! The kingdom of Lesotho is a tiny land-locked nation in the Drakensberg, the eastern part of the Great Escarpment.

HISTORY

People have found **hominin** fossils in northern South African caves that are more than 3 million years old! Over time, humans there formed tribes, such as the Xhosa and Zulu.

In 1652, the Dutch built a fort in southern South Africa. More Dutch settlers arrived. Then, the British set up a colony in this area in 1806. European settlers took land from the African tribes by force.

People in South Africa with Dutch roots were called Boers or Afrikaners.

In 1948, South Africa passed a system of laws called apartheid. It separated white and Black citizens, and allowed white citizens to control aspects of Black citizens' lives. During apartheid, activist Nelson Mandela spent 27 years in prison. After apartheid ended in 1994, he became the country's first Black president. Black and white South Africans have equal rights today.

FACT!
Europeans first sailed around the southern tip of South Africa in 1488.

Protests against apartheid lasted from the 1960s to 1990s.

CRADLE OF HUMANKIND

Northern South Africa has the nickname "Cradle of Humankind" because it holds some of the earliest hominin remains.

GOVERNMENT

South Africa became a republic free from British rule in 1961. A republic is a government in which people elect representatives, or people to work for them in government. The current constitution, or set of laws, was written in 1994.

FACT!
The National Assembly has 400 members, and the National Council has 90 members.

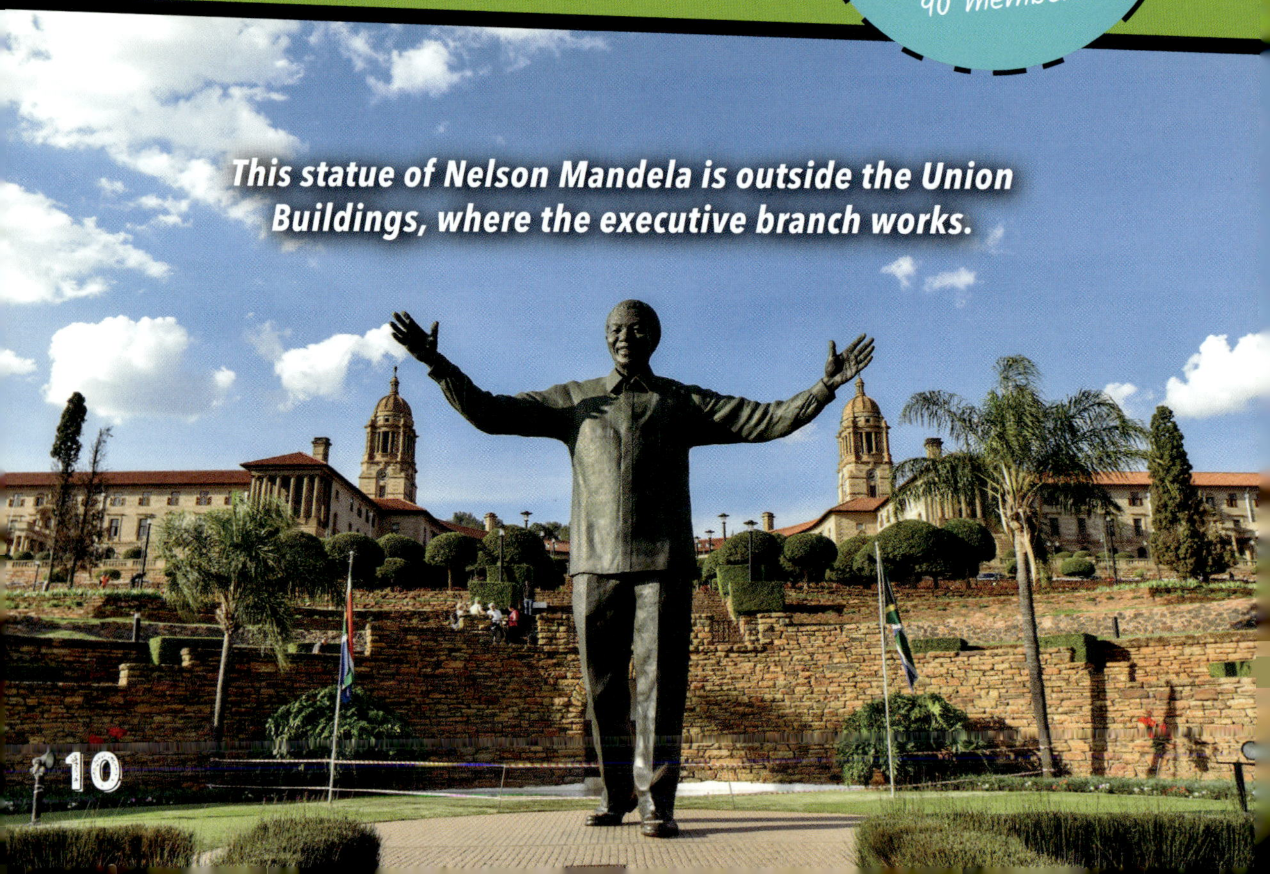

This statue of Nelson Mandela is outside the Union Buildings, where the executive branch works.

South Africa's government has three parts. Parliament is the legislative, or lawmaking, part. It's split into two groups: the National Council and the National Assembly. The executive branch passes new laws, and the president is the head. The courts make up the judicial part of the government. They make sure laws are followed. The executive branch meets in Pretoria, the judiciary meets in Bloemfontein, and Parliament meets in Cape Town. That means South Africa has three capital cities!

EQUAL RIGHTS

The current constitution ensures the equal rights of all South Africans to freedom, respect, and personal safety.

This is where Parliament meets in Cape Town.

THE ECONOMY

An economy is the way a country makes and spends its money. South Africa is the second richest country in Africa, after Nigeria. Mining is one important industry, or group of businesses. Mining started in the 1800s when diamonds and gold were found. After that, many South Africans became miners. The world's largest diamond was found in South Africa. It weighed more than 1 pound (0.45 kilogram). It was cut into several smaller stones. The largest of these is called the Star of Africa.

Another important industry is tourism, or people visiting South Africa. They travel here to see beaches and wild animals. Tourists spend money at eateries, hotels, and other businesses when they stay in South Africa.

RICH AND POOR

A few people in South Africa are very rich, but many more are very poor. It has the highest unemployment, or jobless, rate in the world.

Tourists visit national parks in South Africa to see wild animals.

FACT!

The World Bank called South Africa the most economically unequal country in the world.

South Africa's currency, or unit of money, is the rand.

THE ENVIRONMENT

Many people visit South Africa for its one-of-a-kind natural surroundings, or environment. It is home to nearly 10 percent of the known bird, fish, and plant **species** in the world. Large mammals like zebras, rhinoceroses, and African elephants live here.

FACT!

Illegal, or unlawful, hunting **threatens** many animals, such as the cheetah and black rhinoceros.

Burning coal pollutes the air in South Africa.

PROTECTED LAND AND WATER

South Africa helps the animals and plants that are native to the country by setting aside land and water for them. Wildlife may live safely in dozens of protected areas, such as Kruger National Park.

However, South Africa has many environmental problems. South Africa buries much of its garbage in landfills. These landfills are almost full. This is a big problem.

Another issue is that the land is very dry. Clean, fresh water is hard to find. Air pollution is also a problem. The air is dirty from people driving cars and burning coal for electricity. Mining pollutes both the air and water.

Many species, such as the African forest elephant, suffer from the loss of their habitat, or natural home.

THE PEOPLE TODAY

More than 60 million people live in South Africa today. Around 80 percent of South Africans are Black, while about 8 percent are white. Other groups include people with Indian roots. Some people are of mixed race.

FACT!
The most populated city in South Africa is Johannesburg.

Zulu people practice a **traditional** dance.

People in South Africa don't live as long as people in the United States. People in the United States usually live to be almost 80. People in South Africa usually live only until their mid-60s. One of the reasons for this is the lack of safe drinking water and **sanitation** services for poorer people. Also, many people live with an illness called HIV/AIDS. If left untreated, this illness can spread to others and can cause people to get very sick and even die.

DIFFERENT ETHNIC GROUPS

Some people see all Black South Africans as the same group. However, there are many different groups including the Zulu, Xhosa, Sotho, and Tswana.

A woman collects water in South Africa.

LIFESTYLE

Life is different between cities and the countryside in South Africa. Many people living in the country are farmers. They have a more traditional way of life. In contrast, cities are very modern.

Many people in South Africa are members of a tribe. The largest tribe is the Zulu tribe. The Xhosa tribe is second largest. There are many more tribes. Each tribe has its own traditions and speaks its own language.

These modern apartments sit on the seaside in the city of Durban.

Women in South Africa gained the same rights as men with the most recent constitution. In cities, it's common for both men and women to work outside the home. However, in parts of South Africa, men make many of the decisions and women have traditional roles. This is especially true in the countryside.

FACT!
About 70 percent of South Africa's population lives in urban areas.

STILL UNEQUAL

While white and Black South Africans have the same rights, things are still unequal. The poorest people are mostly Black. Rich South Africans are more likely to be white.

These homes belong to poor people living near Johannesburg.

RELIGION

As with many things in South Africa, religion, or faith, changed when Europeans arrived. Before this, each tribe had its own religion. Some people believed in many gods and goddesses. Others believed in just one god. They had rich traditions and beliefs.

FACT!
South Africa is a secular state. That means it has no national religion that all must follow.

These South African students pray at school.

Europeans forced many people to become Christian when they arrived in South Africa. Today, Christianity is the main religion in South Africa. Many are Methodist or Anglican. A large part of the Black community follows the Zion Christian Church, which mixes Christianity and African traditions. Other South Africans follow Islam, Judaism, and Hinduism. Some follow no religion at all. Religious freedom is granted in the constitution.

KEEPING TRADITIONS ALIVE

If they are sick, many South Africans see a healer called a sangoma or an inyanga. These healers use traditional African religious rituals to cure the sick.

St. George's Cathedral in Cape Town is an Anglican church.

LANGUAGE

Most South Africans can speak more than one language. That's because South Africa has 11 official languages! These are listed in the country's constitution. Most of South Africa's official languages are African languages. They hadn't been written down before Europeans arrived. Today, they're often written with English letters.

DIFFERENT SOUNDS

Some words in African languages use different sounds than English. One of these is a clicking sound.

Cities and areas with lots of tourism often have signs in English.

Some of these languages are spoken more than others. Zulu is spoken the most. Xhosa and Afrikaans are also very popular. Afrikaans is a language that grew out of the Dutch language. Dutch was spoken by many early settlers in South Africa.

English isn't the most common language in South Africa. However, it's the language most used in business and trade.

FACT!

The 11 official languages in the constitution are Afrikaans, English, Ndebele, Pedi, Sotho, Swati, Tsonga, Tswana, Venda, Xhosa, and Zulu.

The Zulu language is the most widely spoken in South Africa.

ARTS AND FESTIVALS

Long before Europeans arrived, South African people created different forms of art, music, and dance. Today, tribes still practice and perform these traditional artforms. There are many festivals to celebrate South African music and dance.

The earliest-known drawing is about 73,000 years old, and it was found in a cave on the southern coast of South Africa.

South Africans have several holidays that celebrate the end of apartheid and honor

FACT!

South African artists sometimes use recycled items like bicycle parts or soda cans in their art.

World-famous comedian Trevor Noah is South African.

Xhosa women perform at the National Arts Festival.

those who fought to end it: They are Human Rights Day (March 21), Freedom Day (April 27), and the Day of **Reconciliation** (December 16).

The National Arts Festival, held in Grahamstown, is the largest arts festival in all of Africa.

THE FATHER OF SOUTH AFRICAN JAZZ

South Africa has been home to many great musicians. Hugh Masekela was a famous jazz trumpeter, singer, and **composer** known as the "father of South African jazz."

FUN AND PLAY

Sports are popular in South Africa. Two of the most popular sports are soccer (called football) and rugby. There are many famous South African players. In 2010, South Africa hosted the FIFA World Cup. That's the most important soccer tournament in the world. It happens once every four years.

Soccer fans cheer at the opening of the FIFA World Cup.

FACT!
South Africans and tourists enjoy spending time on beaches and in parks.

South Africans also like rugby. Under apartheid, usually only white South Africans played and enjoyed rugby. After apartheid, Nelson Mandela worked with the captain of the national rugby team, Francois Pienaar, to use rugby to help bring the nation together. That team won the 1995 Rugby World Cup, which was played in South Africa. Mandela presented the trophy to Pienaar. This moment was an important one in the world of sports—and South African history.

CRICKET

Another popular sport in South Africa is cricket. Cricket is a little bit like baseball. Players use a ball and a bat to play.

South African players celebrate winning the Rugby World Cup in 2007.

FOOD

Different cultures have blended together in the foods of South Africa. Traditional South African food has a lot of vegetables, such as corn. South Africans eat beef, chicken, lamb, and pork. They even eat ostrich! Often, they have friends over for a *braai*. That's another word for barbecue. Meat costs a lot of money. That makes it a special treat for some South Africans.

Bobotie is a popular meal in South Africa.

FACT!

South Africans use corn to make a porridge called mealie pap.

When Europeans came to South Africa, they brought new kinds of food. This included sausages, meat pies, and different types of fish. Indians who moved to South Africa also brought new kinds of food, such as samosas. The food of South Africa highlights the nation's diversity!

A HEALTHY DRINK

South Africans enjoy a special tea called rooibos tea. It is made from the leaves of a plant that grows in the area.

This is a traditional South African braai, or barbecue.

GLOSSARY

archbishop: A bishop, or leader of a church, of the highest rank.

composer: Someone who creates something, especially music.

diversity: The quality or state of having many different types, forms, or ideas.

ethnic: Of or relating to large groups of people who have the same cultural background and ways of life.

hominin: Humans and other species that came before them who walked on two feet.

injustice: A lack of justice or fairness.

peninsula: Land surrounded on three sides by water.

reconciliation: The act of reconciling, or restoring friendship or harmony.

sanitation: A way of keeping places clean from disease, dirt, and other health issues by removing waste and garbage.

savanna: A grassland with scattered patches of trees.

species: A group of plants or animals that are all the same kind.

threaten: To be a cause of loss or harm.

traditional: Having to do with the ways of doing things in a culture that are passed down from parents to children.

FIND OUT MORE

Books

Matthews, Sheelagh. *South Africa*. New York, NY: Lightbox Learning Inc, 2023.

Tyner, Artika R. *Your Passport to South Africa*. North Mankato, MN: Capstone Press, 2023.

Website

South Africa
kids.nationalgeographic.com/geography/countries/article/south-africa
Discover amazing facts about South Africa with *National Geographic Kids*.

Video

African Elephant
www.youtube.com/watch?v=Fk3VdpuFx0Q
Enjoy this funny video about the African elephant from *National Geographic Kids*.

Publisher's note to educators and parents: Our editors have carefully reviewed these websites to ensure that they are suitable for students. Many websites change frequently, however, and we cannot guarantee that a site's future contents will continue to meet our high standards of quality and educational value. Be advised that students should be closely supervised whenever they access the internet.

INDEX